For a brief and terrifying period beginning in late October, 1962, the world stood on the brink of nuclear war. The United States and the Soviet Union faced each other in a confrontation that threatened the existence of mankind. The Russians were placing a large number of missiles in Cuba, capable of blanketing the American continent with nuclear warheads. President John F. Kennedy disclosed the threat in a nationwide television speech on October 22 in which he threw down the gauntlet of battle to Russian Premier Nikita S. Khrushchev. This was a threat that no major nation could accept, he said. Either the Russians would remove the weapons or America would — by force. There followed thirteen days of tense deliberations before Khrushchev finally yielded and the world was spared the horrors of nuclear war.

PRINCIPALS

PRESIDENT JOHN F. KENNEDY, who challenged Premier Khrushchev.

ATTORNEY GENERAL ROBERT F. KENNEDY, the President's brother, who headed the special committee set up to handle the crisis and was largely responsible for the outcome.

SOVIET PREMIER NIKITA S. KHRUSHCHEV, who had pledged never to install offensive weapons in Cuba and who fumed and raged when discovered in the act.

CUBAN PREMIER FIDEL CASTRO, who had established the first Communist regime in the Western Hemisphere and had made the deal with Khrushchev for missile bases.

SOVIET FOREIGN MINISTER ANDREI GROMYKO, who told President Kennedy in the White House that the Russians would never do what the President knew they were doing.

JOHN McCONE, director of the Central Intelligence Agency, who first suspected Russian designs in Cuba.

U.S. AIR FORCE MAJORS RUDOLPH ANDERSON, JR., AND RICHARD C. HEYSER, pilots of the incredibly high-flying U-2 spy plane, who first detected the missile sites.

U.S. JOINT CHIEFS OF STAFF, headed by General Maxwell Taylor — a group that wanted throughout the affair to blast Cuba off the map, insisting the Russians would do nothing.

SECRETARY OF DEFENSE ROBERT McNAMARA, who disagreed, arguing that the U.S. should apply limited pressure first instead of starting at the top of the scale of force.

UNDER SECRETARY OF STATE GEORGE BALL, who also fought the American military position.

U.N. AMBASSADOR ADLAI STEVENSON, who presented the American case to the United Nations and clashed with . . .

SOVIET AMBASSADOR VALERIAN ZORIN, who was subsequently routed in the heated exchange.

Tension mounts in the Cuban missile crisis as President John F. Kennedy signs the proclamation formally putting into effect at 10:00 A.M. the following morning the United States arms quarantine against Cuba. It was the evening of October 23, 1962, and the President signed the document without comment. (UPI Photo)

THE CUBAN MISSILE CRISIS

OCTOBER 1962
The U.S. and Russia
Face a Nuclear Showdown

By Fred J. Cook

A World Focus Book

FRANKLIN WATTS, INC.
NEW YORK, 1972

Library of Congress Cataloging in Publication Data

Cook, Fred J
    The Cuban missile crisis October 1962.

    (A World focus book)
    SUMMARY: Describes the events that precipi-
tated the 1962 Cuban missile crisis and analyzes the
steps taken by President Kennedy to avert the threat
to the security of the western hemisphere.
    1. Military bases, Russian — Cuba — Juvenile
literature. 2. U. S.—Foreign relations—Russia—Juvenile literature. 3. Russia—Foreign relations—U. S.
—Juvenile literature. 4. Cuba—History—1959- —
Juvenile literature. [1. Cuba—History—1959-
2. U. S.—Foreign relations—Russia. 3. Russia—
Foreign relations—U. S.] I. Title.
E183.8.R9C62   327.73'047   72-696
ISBN 0-531-02159-9

Contents

President Kennedy reports to the American people over nationwide tele-vision on October 22, 1962, from the White House. His message: the Soviet Union was installing nuclear weapons in Cuba. (UPI Photo)

Eyeball to Eyeball

It was the night of October 22, 1962 — a night when a shudder of horror ran across the nation and, indeed, across a large part of the civilized world. For it was a night when man, for the first time in human history, was brought face to face with the possibility that he and his world might cease to exist on the morrow.

United States President John F. Kennedy, young, handsome, stern-faced, was addressing the nation on television. His message: the Soviet Union was installing nuclear weapons in Cuba, just 90 miles from American shores.

It was an act of recklessness and deceit that few had expected. The world had lived under the shadow of nuclear terror ever since America had exploded the first atom bomb above Hiroshima, Japan, in World War II. But until this moment, it had been only that — a shadow — not a hideous, imminent reality that might, in an hour's time, turn most of the planet into a charred, radioactive crisp.

After the Soviets developed nuclear weapons and the long-range missiles to deliver them, they had seemed to realize that they possessed a destructive force so horrible it must be tightly guarded. They had never entrusted nuclear weapons to the Communist Chinese, or to the Communist Poles, or to any of their other satellite powers. They had kept such weapons under tight control within the Soviet Union; they had vowed that they always would — and the world had believed them.

1

But now, in an act of incredible daring, Soviet Premier Nikita S. Khrushchev had placed offensive missiles and their nuclear warheads in Cuba, where Fidel Castro had established a Communist regime. By this act, Khrushchev had changed all the rules of the game and had upset the delicate balance of deterrent nuclear weaponry. As a result, the United States and Russia — the two powers that possessed nuclear arsenals capable of destroying the entire world — stood "eyeball to eyeball" in a confrontation menacing the very existence of man.

President Kennedy, in words that were firm, controlled, and yet terrifying, spelled out the deceit and the menace. He had first received hard evidence of Russian missiles in Cuba at 9 A.M. the previous Tuesday, October 16. This evidence had since been confirmed and reevaluated, and the steps America would take to meet this new threat had already been determined. The President said that the nation was faced with a crisis because the Russian bases in Cuba menaced the entire Western Hemisphere.

The President further pointed out that medium-range ballistic missiles that could carry a nuclear warhead 1,000 miles were "capable of striking Washington, D.C., the Panama Canal, Cape Canaveral, Mexico City, or any other city in the southeastern part of the United States, in Central America, or in the Caribbean area."

Even more menacing was the fact that the Soviets were building bases and launching pads for even longer-range, intermediate missiles that could lay waste targets "as far north as Hudson Bay, Canada, and as far south as Lima, Peru." They were also uncrating and assembling jet bombers capable of adding to the potential nuclear barrage.

The President, his face grim, his right arm and forefinger

Soviet Premier Nikita Khrushchev in a typical pose, Paris, 1960. He took this occasion to attack the Eisenhower administration on the U-2 spy flight incident. (UPI Photo)

thrusting and jabbing to emphasize his points, denounced the Soviets for introducing "offensive weapons of sudden mass destruction" into Cuba — and for the lies and deceit that had accompanied the move.

Kennedy spelled out in scathing terms the number of times the Soviet government had given solemn assurances that it would never attempt to set up strategic nuclear bases outside its own territory. After describing each pledge, the President jabbed with his forefinger and said: "That statement was false."

He also declared that "this secret, swift, and extraordinary buildup of Communist missiles" in Cuba was "a deliberately provocative and unjustified change in the status quo which cannot be accepted by this country if our courage and our commitments are ever to be trusted again by either friend or foe."

Therefore, the President said, he had determined upon a course of action. The United States would throw "a strict quarantine on all offensive military equipment under shipment to Cuba," and the navy would stop and turn back any cargo ships carrying such weapons. We were stepping up our aerial surveillance of Cuba, and we were beefing up our armed forces in the southeastern United States "to prepare for any eventualities." If the Soviets persisted in going ahead with their nuclear buildup, "further action will be justified" — in other words, all-out war might well result.

The President hoped, of course, to avoid this. He stressed that we were taking steps on the diplomatic front. We were asking for the support of the nations of the Western Hemisphere represented by the Organization of American States, and we were calling for "an emergency meeting" of the United Nations Security Council to act "against this latest Soviet threat to world

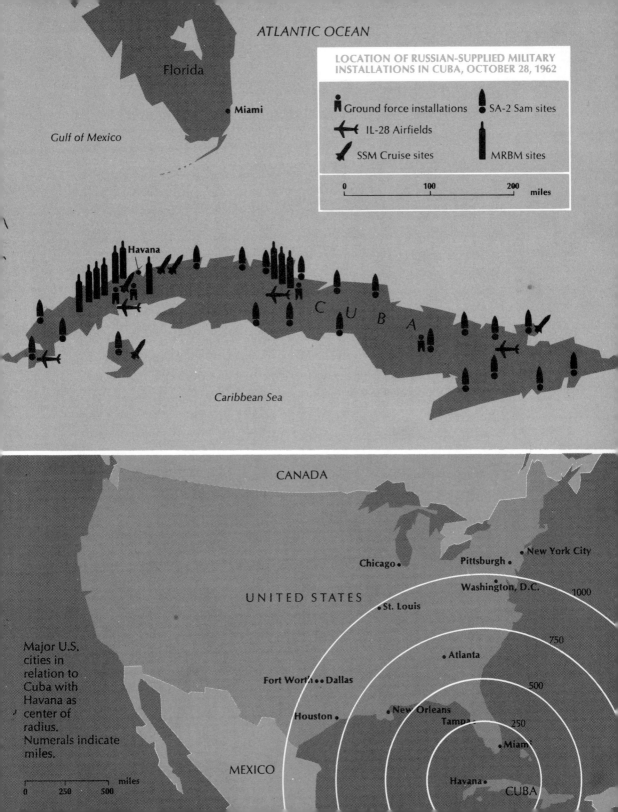

ATLANTIC OCEAN

Florida

Miami

Gulf of Mexico

LOCATION OF RUSSIAN-SUPPLIED MILITARY
INSTALLATIONS IN CUBA, OCTOBER 28, 1962

Ground force installations   SA-2 Sam sites

IL-28 Airfields   MRBM sites

SSM Cruise sites

0   100   200   miles

Havana

C U B A

Caribbean Sea

CANADA

New York City

Chicago   Pittsburgh

Washington, D.C.   1000

UNITED STATES

St. Louis

750

Atlanta

Major U.S.
cities in
relation to
Cuba with
Havana as
center of
radius.
Numerals indicate
miles.

Fort Worth Dallas   500

Houston   New Orleans

Tampa   250

Miami

MEXICO

Havana   CUBA

0   250   500   miles

peace." The United States, the President said, would insist before the U.N. on "the prompt dismantling and withdrawal of all offensive weapons in Cuba, under the supervision of United Nations observers. . . ."

If this was not done, the American nation and, indeed, the world clearly stood on the brink of nuclear war. The President put the issue in one blunt, chilling sentence. He said: "It shall be the policy of this nation to regard any missile launched from Cuba against any nation in the Western Hemisphere as an attack by the Soviet Union on the United States, requiring a full retaliatory response upon the Soviet Union."

In other words, the firing of the first missile from Cuba would trigger a nuclear bombardment that would kill untold millions of people in both the Soviet Union and the United States, and that would subject much of the rest of the world to an unprecedented and deadly radioactive deluge. Thus it was clear that the two giants of the nuclear age faced each other with the fate of man and civilization in the balance, and no one could foretell the outcome.

In the last of his stipulated conditions, President Kennedy pleaded with Premier Khrushchev to draw back from the brink — "to halt and eliminate this clandestine, reckless, and provocative threat to world peace and to stable relations between our two nations."

But would Khrushchev, who had gambled so recklessly, be in any position to heed this voice of reason? With his own and his nation's prestige at stake, could he afford to? Would the military hard-liners in his own government let him?

Those were the crucial questions. And the whole world trembled while it waited for the answers.

The Background of the Missile Crisis

How had it happened? How had it come about that the two mightiest nations of the atomic age had been brought into head-on confrontation over a Caribbean island of only 44,218 square miles, inhabited by a mere seven million people?

The seeds had been sown in the revolution that had put Fidel Castro in power and established the first Communist regime in the Western Hemisphere. Castro, who had landed on the Cuban coast with only a handful of followers, had capitalized on popular revolt against the brutal dictatorship of Fulgencio Batista. When Batista fled the country on January 1, 1959, Cubans danced in the streets, believing they were free at last.

Their joy was short-lived, however. It soon became apparent that Castro's regime was dominated by Communists. And Castro himself began to seize foreign-owned enterprises, to carve up the great plantations, and to communize the sugarcane fields. Having turned Cuba into a Communist state, he tried to spread his ideology to other nations of Central and South America. But here Castro failed, and Cuba gradually became ever more isolated in the Western Hemisphere — and ever more dependent on the Soviet Union.

The establishment and continued existence of Castro's Communist rule in Cuba, however, shocked and alarmed Americans. The Republican administration of President Dwight D.

7

(Above) Fidel Castro enters Havana in triumph after successfully ousting the dictator Batista, January 1, 1959. (Below) Cuban refugees arriving in Florida, 1960. Some were escapees from Havana's Morro Castle prison. (UPI Photos)

Eisenhower cut off all trade and other relations with Cuba and slowly began to lay plans for the overthrow of Castro.

Some one hundred thousand Cuban refugees had already crowded into the Miami area. Among them were followers of Batista, who had fled from Cuba with their brutal master. Others were professional men — doctors, lawyers, teachers — who had found Castro's tyrannical regime insupportable. Still others were former followers of Castro, men of principle who had believed they were taking part in a true, democratic revolution, but who had discovered too late that they had been mere pawns in a Communist game.

Many of these Cubans had two things in common: a love of their homeland to which they desired to return, and a hatred of Castro. They dreamed of participating in another revolution that would oust the new dictator. For Americans, who detested the very thought of communism, these Cubans represented a heaven-sent force.

The Central Intelligence Agency — the information-gathering arm of the government that has often played a dual role in overthrowing radical regimes Americans do not like — began to recruit Cuban refugees and to toy with the idea of arming them for the overthrow of Castro. The CIA had worked just such a subtle miracle in Guatemala in 1954, when it toppled the pro-Communist government of Jacobo Arbenz and replaced it with its own hand-picked, militaristic administration. The CIA was confident it could repeat this success in Cuba.

Under pressure to "do something" about Cuba, President Eisenhower on March 17, 1960, authorized the CIA to organize, train, and equip Cuban refugees as anti-Castro guerrillas. The

CIA set up training camps in the Guatemalan jungles, and soon some fifteen hundred Cubans were being drilled there.

President Eisenhower himself later said that he never planned or contemplated a full-scale invasion of Cuba. He apparently thought that the guerrillas would be landed on the Cuban coast much as Castro himself had landed, and would be used for the kind of hit-and-run warfare that might spark an internal revolt in Cuba. No one has ever questioned Eisenhower's veracity, but what has been questioned is his leadership. It seems obvious that he lost control of the project he set in motion by his March, 1960, authorization to the CIA.

There were several reasons for this. Throughout his presidency, Eisenhower preferred to delegate authority. He made broad decisions, then left them to others to carry out, sometimes keeping little check upon them. In addition, in 1960, he was not a healthy man. He had suffered a major heart attack and had undergone major operations. Understandably, his White House staff became protective and shielded him as much as possible from vexing problems. As a result, there developed a kind of vacuum in which the CIA became a law unto itself, formulating an aggressive policy that would drag the entire nation after it.

Unknown to authorities in Washington, guerrilla training in the Guatemalan camps was stopped and emphasis was shifted to preparations for a full-scale invasion. The spearhead of the planned assault on Castro's citadel would be the Cuban brigade of fifteen hundred men, aided by World War II planes flown from Guatemala by paid fliers; and if this did not prove to be enough, the Cubans were assured that American naval and air power would be available to support them.

The evidence indicates that these pledges of American com-

Cuban exiles training as anti-Castro guerrilla troops in Guatemala, 1961. (UPI Photo)

mitment were made by the CIA independent of any decision on the national level in Washington. What had happened was that the CIA was dealing itself an independent hand, regardless of the desires of the national government it was supposed to serve.

This was the situation, the secret CIA plans complete and

snowballing and the invasion ready to roll, when John F. Kennedy took office in January, 1961. The young President found himself in a difficult position. In the 1960 election campaign, in the fourth of his series of televised debates with Vice-President Richard M. Nixon, he had tried to make political capital out of the Cuban situation, denouncing the Republican Eisenhower administration for permitting the establishment of a Communist base only 90 miles off our shores. By so doing he had, in effect, committed himself to action against Castro; and now, in the first days of his presidency, his hand was called. He was presented with a completed plan.

Central Intelligence Agency chief Allen Dulles with President Kennedy at Hyannis Port, Massachusetts, July, 1960. (UPI Photo)

Kennedy hesitated. He was wise enough to realize that there would be a furious backlash of world opinion if the mighty United States hurled its armed forces against tiny Cuba. This smacked too much of the old-fashioned "gunboat diplomacy" of the early 1900's that had aroused much of South America against the United States. Yet if Kennedy backed down, he would certainly be subjected, as his Democratic predecessors had been, to Republican charges that he was "soft on Communism." Furthermore, he was no military expert, and the Cuban invasion plans had been perfected during the administration of Dwight Eisenhower, the nation's most revered general. Who was he to question them?

In addition, his advisers were almost unanimous in telling him it would be quite easy. Allen Dulles, chief of the CIA, stood by the presidential desk and assured the worried Kennedy that the overthrow of Castro would be easier than the 1954 coup that had ousted Arbenz in Guatemala. The Joint Chiefs of Staff, the nation's top military experts, backed the venture to a man. Only Senator J. William Fulbright of Arkansas, chairman of the Senate Foreign Relations Committee, vigorously denounced the scheme as unworthy of America and hostile to the most vital American ideals and traditions. But his was a lonely voice, quickly overborne by the chorus of experts, one of whom cried confidently at the final White House conference, "Let 'er rip!" The disaster of the Bay of Pigs followed.

On April 17, 1961, the CIA-trained Cuban brigade was put ashore in a tidal marshland on the southern shore of Cuba. The weak aerial bombardment that had preceded the invasion had failed to knock out Castro's puny air force, and the dictator's remaining planes strafed the invaders and attacked their supply

13

Aftermath of the abortive Bay of Pigs invasion by anti-Castro forces. Successful defending troops inspect a knocked-out tank at Giron Beach, April, 1961. (UPI Photo)

ships. Unknown to the attacking Cubans — who had been promised American support by the CIA — in giving his final approval to the venture President Kennedy had decreed that it must be a completely Cuban operation. American power and prestige were not to be committed.

With the Cuban brigade bogged down in the Bay of Pigs marshes and under fierce attack by Castro's land and air forces, the President came under intense pressure from the military to rescind his original order and unleash American armed might. He refused. The result was a debacle. Castro wiped out the helpless invaders, rounding up some twelve hundred prisoners and killing the rest.

The whole bungled adventure had been an American disaster and disgrace, and it profoundly affected the course of future events. Studying the record later, many were to conclude that it was probably the sorry Bay of Pigs affair that later led the Russians to gamble on installing missiles in Cuba.

Premier Khrushchev, a hard man, believed that a great nation was supposed to use its full power when its interests were challenged. He had not hesitated in 1956 when an uprising in Hungary threatened his puppet regime there; he had crushed the revolt ruthlessly with Red Army tanks and firepower. Moreover, he viewed with ill-concealed contempt the actions of an American President who had been too squeamish over principles to follow a similar course when disaster threatened at the Bay of Pigs.

Khrushchev's attitude became apparent at his summit meeting with President Kennedy in Vienna, Austria, in early June, 1961. The Russian premier bullied Kennedy about the Bay of Pigs failure, and Kennedy snapped back, wondering if the Russians had never made any mistakes themselves. The President came out of the confrontation grim-faced and seething — and determined to show the Russians how tough he could be.

Even some of his own close associates and admirers would concede later that he probably over-reacted to the Khrushchev bullyragging at Vienna. In the fall of 1961, he called up the National Guard to meet a supposed Khrushchev threat to encircled Berlin, only to find there was nothing for the guard to do.

Cuban Premier Castro and Soviet Premier Khrushchev confer in mid-1962.
(UPI Photo)

He also stepped up the American commitment to South Vietnam, helping to set the nation on the course that would bog it down in a costly and futile war.

These moves, however, seem to have had little effect on Khrushchev. The Russian premier evidently felt that in the face-to-face Vienna meeting he had taken the measure of his man. Thus he remained convinced that he was dealing with a young, uncertain President whom he could push around with impunity. He did not appreciate the tough underlying fiber of the Kennedys — and this was his first, colossal miscalculation.

Mysterious Developments

The month of July, 1962, was marked by a number of mysterious developments. On July 2, Raul Castro, brother of Fidel and Cuba's defense minister, arrived in Moscow on an unexplained mission. He conferred with Khrushchev, and by the end of the month American intelligence became worried about some strange doings on the high seas.

A stream of Soviet ships put out from Baltic and Black Sea ports, all headed for Cuba. Some of these vessels were lumber-trade freighters with exceptionally wide hatches, and they seemed to ride high in the water. It was assumed at the time that the Russians, having committed themselves fully to Castro, had rounded up whatever shipping was available to supply Cuba. Only later would it become apparent that there was another explanation for the use of these wide-hatched, high-riding ships. Missiles are bulky objects, requiring wide hatches for stowing purposes; but they are not so heavy that they weigh a vessel down in the water.

American intelligence, keeping track of this sudden flow of seaborne aid to Castro, spotted most of the Russian ships docking in the port of Mariel on the north coast of Cuba. The CIA learned that the port had been transformed. That is, Cubans living near the wharves had been moved out, and Russian sentries patrolled the docks while Russian sailors and longshoremen unloaded the cargoes. What was going on?

Aerial photo shows a Soviet ship inbound for Cuba with jet bomber fuselage crates on the decks. Photo was taken in October, 1962, by U.S. reconnaissance aircraft. (UPI Photo)

At the time, this activity was a great puzzle. Roger Hilsman, then director of intelligence and research for the State Department, gave reporters a background briefing on August 24. He said that eight Soviet-bloc ships had docked in Cuba between July 26 and August 8, and perhaps a dozen more had arrived between August 9 and 24. Between three thousand and five thousand Soviet technicians had been landed, and American intelligence had determined that large quantities of transportation, electronic, and construction equipment had been poured ashore. The conclusion was that Russia was beefing up Castro's air de-

CHERRY PICKER

XIDIZER TRAILERS

2 FUEL TRAILERS

METALLURG ANOSOV

TRAILERS

MISSILE ERECTOR

DIVNOGORSK

BRATSK

A revealing low-level aerial shot of the naval port at Mariel, Cuba, showing missile trailers and other equipment. Russian buildup began here in the summer of 1962. Photo, taken in November, shows Russian ships ready to move out the equipment. (Photo from Cushing)

fense to guard against another invasion attempt like the Bay of Pigs.

Only John McCone, a Republican who had replaced Allen Dulles as head of the CIA, seems to have had serious doubts. In a discussion with President Kennedy two days before the Hilsman briefing, he speculated that the Russians might be introducing offensive missiles into Cuba. Admittedly, McCone had no evidence; he was guessing — but he was guessing shrewdly.

His reasoning went like this: surface-to-air missiles (SAMs) could hardly deter an invasion, but they would be invaluable in protecting offensive missile sites. To the argument that the Russians had never yet trusted their puppets with nuclear weapons, McCone had an answer. Missiles with a range of 1,000 miles, he said — if they were placed in Poland or Hungary — could be turned around to menace Russia if the Communist governments in those countries fell; but 1,000-mile-range missiles, if placed in Cuba, could never threaten Russia, no matter what happened.

McCone's guesses would seem brilliant later, but at the moment even he did not take the situation too seriously. A widower who had recently remarried, he went off on a honeymoon trip to Europe shortly after his talk with Kennedy, leaving behind him an increasingly ticklish situation.

In early September, American intelligence agencies began to get a stream of reports from refugee channels that still had contacts inside Cuba. The main theme of these reports was startling: the Russians were assembling not only the SAM (surface-to-air) missiles, but longer-range (surface-to-surface) missiles capable of striking American cities with nuclear warheads.

Still, the American intelligence community was skeptical of these reports. It had learned from past experience that refugees' tales were often unreliable, some seeming at times to have been deliberately manufactured in the hope of embroiling the United States with Castro. In addition, intelligence agents questioned whether untutored Cubans on the scene knew enough about missiles to be able to distinguish between a SAM and longer-range weapons.

No such commonsense reserve deterred the Republicans, however. The midterm Congressional election campaign of 1962 was heating up, and the Republicans' great issue was the failure of the Kennedy administration to do something about Cuba. The white-maned Republican senator from New York, Kenneth Keating, took the Senate floor in a series of slashing speeches declaring that he had positive information that the Russians

Soviet Ambassador Anatoly Dobrynin. (Wide World)

were installing offensive missiles in Cuba. Keating apparently was relying on the kind of refugee reports intelligence agencies considered suspect, but when the administration asked him to identify his sources and help it confirm the information, he refused.

With the domestic political pot boiling in this heated fashion, the Russians now embarked on a program of calculated deceit. On September 4, Khrushchev sent the Soviet ambassador to Washington, Anatoly Dobrynin, to call on the President's brother, Attorney General Robert F. Kennedy. Dobrynin said that he carried a special message from Khrushchev to the President for transmission only through the attorney general: the Russian premier pledged that he would do nothing to embarrass

Attorney General Robert F. Kennedy. (UPI Photo)

the Kennedy administration during the election campaign. When Robert Kennedy pressed Dobrynin about the arms buildup in Cuba, the ambassador assured him that Russia would never place in the hands of a third party weapons that might involve the Soviet Union in thermonuclear war.

Robert Kennedy, hardheaded and skeptical, was not satisfied. He suggested to his brother that it was time to draft a flat, public warning to the Russians. President Kennedy agreed and later that same day issued a statement warning that the introduction of offensive missiles into Cuba would precipitate a grave crisis. He also pledged himself to prevent, by whatever means might be necessary, any armed action by Castro against any nation in the Western Hemisphere.

Moscow replied by dipping deeper into its bag of deceit. On September 11 the Kremlin said flatly that the "armaments and military equipment sent to Cuba are designed exclusively for defensive purposes." It added:

"There is no need for the Soviet Union to shift its weapons for the repulsion of aggression, for a retaliatory blow, to any other country, for instance Cuba. Our nuclear weapons are so powerful in their explosive force and the Soviet Union has such powerful rockets to carry these nuclear warheads, that there is no need to search for sites for them beyond the boundaries of the Soviet Union."

No assurance could have been more explicit. No assurance could have been more false.

Two days later, in his September 13 press conference, President Kennedy took note of the Russian statement and issued a further, more explicit warning. He said that our information indicated the Russian shipments to Cuba did not constitute a serious threat at this time, but he added pointedly that, if Cuba were ever to become "an offensive military base of significant capacity for the Soviet Union, then this country will do whatever must be done to protect its own security and that of its allies."

In these statements the battle lines for the coming collision were clearly drawn. All that remained to produce the crisis was the exposure of Russian duplicity. And it was at this stage of the deadly game that a most unusual American spy plane, the U-2, furnished the United States with conclusive evidence of what was going on in Cuba.

An Air Force U-2 aircraft in flight on a reconnaissance mission. (Wide World)

The U-2 has a stubby fuselage 49½ feet long. It has tapering, gliderlike wings that stretch 80 feet across. It can fly at enormous altitudes, 14 miles or higher, and it is equipped with phenomenal cameras focused through seven portholes in its belly. These cameras can photograph a sweep of the earth 125 miles wide and 3,000 miles long as the high-flying, almost invisible bird swoops above hostile territory. In fact, the lenses of these cameras are so sharp that, under ideal conditions, they can photograph a readable newspaper headline from 8 or 10 miles up in the air.

The U-2s are so crammed with photographic equipment that they cannot be burdened with such extra-weight items as landing gear. They take off from a detachable dolly; and when they return to base, the tips of their gliderlike wings shorten and bend down and they come skidding in like a sled on their reinforced bellies.

President Kennedy had relied more and more on the U-2s as the mysterious Russian buildup in Cuba continued. He had doubled the number of flights over Castro's island empire, but the flights of September and early October had spotted nothing of an alarming character. They showed that the Russian installations were being developed with incredible rapidity, but they seemed to be strictly defensive in character.

CIA Director John McCone, back from his wedding trip in early October, discovered that most of these spy flights had concentrated on the Cuban coast east of Havana. He argued forcefully that greater attention should be paid to the western end of the island. At the same time, intelligence experts discovered what appeared to them to be a significant arrangement of SAM sites around San Cristobal — an arrangement remarkably similar to

Two aerial photos of the San Cristobal area of Cuba. Upper photo was taken on October 14, showing a Soviet medium-range ballistic missile unit had moved in with erectors, trailers, and other equipment. Photo below was taken October 23 and indicates tempo of Soviet activity has increased with additional equipment introduced into the area. (UPI Photos)

patterns previously photographed in Russia, where SAMs were concentrated around missile sites.

Therefore, a decision was made to concentrate on San Cristobal and the western tip of Cuba. But now bad weather intervened. The U-2s lose much of their effectiveness if the sky is as much as 25 percent overcast, and so the planes had to wait for clearing weather. Finally, on October 14, weather conditions were right, and two U-2s piloted by Air Force Majors Rudolph Anderson, Jr., of Spartanburg, South Carolina, and Richard C. Heyser, of Battle Creek, Michigan, took off for their high-altitude sweep over western Cuba.

Anderson and Heyser had been warned that they might draw antiaircraft fire from the SAMs, but the guns below remained silent throughout their mission. Late in the day, after a routine flight, they skidded back down on their landing field. Then the film magazines were whisked out of their planes and flown to Washington for development and evaluation.

There, all of the following day, Monday, October 15, photographic experts studied the thousands of frames produced by the fast-rolling U-2 cameras. Late in the day they discovered the evidence that would bring the world to the brink of nuclear war. In a field enclosed by woods near San Cristobal, the hawk-eyed cameras had photographed missile erectors, launchers, and transporters — all the paraphernalia of an offensive ballistic missile system in the process of erection.

It was this discovery that led to the great confrontation between nuclear powers — to thirteen days of tension and drama of a type unsurpassed in American history.

First Discussions

That same Monday night, telephones began to ring all over Washington as intelligence experts alerted members of the Kennedy administration to the discovery that had been made at San Cristobal. Key administration officials who received these calls were almost all at one function or another, some at private parties, others at state dinners with foreign diplomats. One by one, after they got the word, they returned quietly to whatever function it was they were attending and tried to join in lighthearted conversation — as if they had not the faintest inkling of the approaching crisis that might well determine the fate of the world.

McGeorge Bundy, the White House special assistant for

McGeorge Bundy, White House special assistant for national security affairs. (Wide World)

President Kennedy poses with Charles E. Bohlen, White House adviser and former ambassador to Russia, on porch outside President's office. (Wide World)

national security affairs, was told of the San Cristobal findings in an 8:30 P.M. telephone call from Deputy CIA Director Ray Cline. The news came at a most awkward time for Bundy. He was giving a dinner party in his home for Charles E. Bohlen, the newly appointed ambassador to France. Among the guests were members of the French Embassy and at least one Washington reporter. Bundy wondered what he should do. If he walked out on his own dinner party, gossipy Washington would sense in an instant that some earthshaking crisis was at hand. This was unthinkable, Bundy decided. Besides, he could almost hear President Kennedy's first question: "Is the evidence hard enough to go on?" It would take intelligence experts all night working on their pictures, blowing up the key telltale frames, to answer that question convincingly. "I decided the bad news could wait until Tuesday morning," Bundy said later.

At 8 A.M. on Tuesday he met in his little basement office in the White House with an intelligence officer and two photo-analysts. Bundy studied the photographs they showed him and read an accompanying intelligence report. Then, convinced the evidence was solid, he took the elevator to Kennedy's living quarters and found the President sitting on the edge of his bed in pajamas and dressing gown, reading the morning newspapers.

"Mr. President," Bundy said, "there is now hard photographic evidence, which you will see later, that the Russians have offensive missiles in Cuba."

After the first moment of shock, the President moved swiftly. He ordered Bundy to call a strictly secret meeting at 11:45 A.M. of a select list of advisers whose opinions he wanted. He ticked off the names: Vice-President Lyndon B. Johnson; Secretary of State Dean Rusk; Secretary of Defense Robert McNamara; Attorney General Kennedy; General Maxwell Taylor, Chairman of the Joint Chiefs of Staff; General Marshall S. Carter, McCone's deputy in the CIA; Roswell Gilpatric, Deputy Secretary of Defense; George Ball, Under Secretary of State; Edwin M. Martin, Assistant Secretary of State for Inter-American

31

Affairs; Bundy; Theodore Sorensen, long-time Kennedy aide and special assistant to the President; Treasury Secretary Douglas Dillon; Ambassador Bohlen; and Kenneth O'Donnell, the President's appointments secretary.

The membership of this elite group would change a bit from day to day as others whom the President trusted and respected

Top leaders of the soon-to-be-set-up National Security Council arrive for a secret meeting during the Cuban missile crisis. From left: Vice-President Lyndon B. Johnson; CIA Director John McCone; and Under Secretary of State George Ball. (UPI Photo)

would be called in for their advice; but these were the men who were to bear the bulk of an awesome responsibility — deciding on a course of action that would counter the Russian threat without triggering a nuclear holocaust.

President Kennedy, having set this machinery of consultation in motion, next telephoned the man on whom he relied most heavily in any crisis, his brother, Robert. Robert Kennedy later recalled that the President spoke to him shortly after 9 A.M. and asked him to come at once to the White House. "He said only that we were facing great trouble," Robert Kennedy wrote later.

At the White House, the President quickly brought his brother up-to-date on the U-2 photographic discoveries. Robert Kennedy at once realized that the United States and Russia were involved in a confrontation "which brought the world to the abyss of nuclear destruction and the end of mankind."

The group of men whom President Kennedy had designated, with the President himself presiding, assembled in the Cabinet Room at 11:45 on this first morning of crisis to consider what should be done. The group was to become known later as the Executive Committee of the National Security Council, or Ex-Com. From the moment it first assembled it was to meet two or three times a day as its members, working themselves to the brink of mental and physical exhaustion, weighed the facts and argued, debated, fought over the best course to follow.

Robert Kennedy later recalled that, at this first meeting, "the dominant feeling was one of shocked incredulity." No one had expected Khrushchev to take so foolhardy a step. Why had he gambled so desperately?

Several of those present thought that Khrushchev's Cuban gambit might be related to Berlin. For fifteen months, the Rus-

33

Together during the October crisis. President Kennedy (right) confers with his brother Robert F. Kennedy at the White House. (Wide World)

sian premier had been trying to force the Western powers out of the former German capital. The Cuban missiles might represent his trump card. It was not too difficult to imagine this scenario: Khrushchev would wait until after the American elections. Then he would spring his surprise. He would appear suddenly before the United Nations. He would disclose the existence of his Cuban arsenal and offer the West this choice: "Get out of Berlin if you want us to take our missiles out of Cuba."

This, of course, would be bald-faced blackmail. What should the United States do to prevent it? There were a few, a very few, around the table in the conference room who suggested that the presence of missiles in Cuba did not greatly change the strategic situation. Robert McNamara, for example, at first took the attitude that "a missile is a missile" and that it did not matter greatly whether cities were incinerated by missiles fired from Russia or Cuba. The result would be the same. This, however, was a minority view. Most of those there saw the Russian move as a naked threat of force that upset the strategic balance in the world — a threat that must be met head-on.

Although there was general agreement that something must be done, there was none on what the specific steps should be. Even at this first session, the conferees began to split into two groups that were later to be dubbed "hawks" and "doves." The first group, led by the military, wanted to "take out" the Cuban missile sites in a surprise air strike as quickly as possible; the "doves," reminding the "hawks" that such action would involve the slaughter of a lot of Russians and Cubans, feared that Russia would be driven to violent reaction and that the result would be nuclear war. They argued that we should take some less drastic first step, one that would be forceful enough to make our determination clear, but one that would give Khrushchev time to look into the chamber of nuclear horrors, to reflect, and possibly to pull back with whatever face-saving grace he could muster.

From the beginning until the end — and even after a decision had been reached — the struggle between these two groups was often fierce and bitter. The Joint Chiefs of Staff and their hard-line civilian cohorts were never to be reconciled to any policy except the use of brute force. From the first, their attitude shocked Robert Kennedy, who scribbled a note and passed it to his brother. The note read: "I now know how Tojo felt when he was planning Pearl Harbor."

After the meeting in the Cabinet Room, the President and his brother walked back together to the White House. The President, worried and thoughtful, told his brother that he would not attend all future meetings of ExCom for two reasons. The first was that he wanted to maintain appearances: he wished to keep up his normal public schedule in order not to arouse suspicion that so much was known before a course of action had been decided on. Secondly, he wanted the freest possible discussion to take place among his advisers — the kind of give-and-take debate leading to a proposal of alternatives that, JFK realized, can rarely take place in the presence of the President, whose power and prestige influences men and tends to make them modify their own ideas to suit what they sense are his wishes.

From this first tense meeting, then, there had emerged just one cardinal decision: President Kennedy would not sit still; he would act. However, the nature of that action had yet to be determined.

Robert Kennedy
Takes Charge

With the President absent from many of these ExCom meetings, Robert Kennedy now took charge of this "think tank" where the future was being decided. Although he was the youngest man in the room (not quite 37) and outranked by others (even though he was the President's brother), Robert Kennedy soon became the leader of them all.

Vice-President Johnson sat on the sidelines. Participants in the discussions later agreed that he played no decisive role. He seldom spoke unless spoken to; he offered no advice. Secretary of State Dean Rusk was the ranking Cabinet officer among those taking part in the deliberations, which were now being held in George Ball's conference room in the State Department. As host and chief Cabinet officer, Rusk might have been expected to assume the role of chairman, but he did not. For days, none of those present knew where he stood, and the wisecrack later went around Washington that Rusk had been both "a hove and a dawk."

In this vacuum, Robert Kennedy swiftly became the unofficial chairman — the discussion leader. He was careful in the beginning not to indicate how he himself felt. In fact, he played the role of devil's advocate, often asking sharp and leading questions. He deferred to no man's age, rank, or reputation. He attacked every opinion and made the man who advocated it de-

Attorney General Kennedy, who swiftly became the unofficial leader of the newly formed National Security Council, is shown here leaving a top secret meeting. (Wide World)

fend it. Some felt he was rude. Some of the much older men resented this rough handling by what they considered a mere stripling.

U.N. Ambassador Adlai Stevenson, after he joined the discussions, reacted to the younger Kennedy with strong distaste. The attorney general, he said, acted like "a bull in a china shop." But, in the end, even Stevenson had to admit that Robert Kennedy had been the strongest man in the room and that the prudent course finally adopted was to a great degree the latter's handiwork.

The Specter of Nuclear Disaster

A grim shadow hovered above the shoulders of all these men during the tense days of debate. This was the specter of possible nuclear disaster. Although the vast majority of the American people still did not realize it, nuclear weaponry had advanced to the stage where its use could no longer really protect mankind but could only hasten its obliteration.

The atom bomb with which the United States had wiped out Hiroshima in 1945, killing some one hundred thousand persons in a few blinding seconds, had been a primitive device — little more than a shotgun blast in the approaching age of nuclear cannon. Later, in the mid-1950s, the atom bomb had given way to the hydrogen bomb. The Hiroshima weapon had had a force of 20,000 tons of TNT; but nuclear force was now measured not in thousands of tons — but in millions, or *megatons.*

Thus a 10-megaton bomb packed an explosive force 500 times as great as the A-bomb that had leveled Hiroshima, but even a 10-megaton bomb was still rather small in the modern nuclear arsenal. The big weapons measured as much as 40 megatons, and the Russians had even exploded a 50–60 megaton device. The explosion of just one of these larger bombs high above the American heartland could not only wipe out an entire city like Chicago; it could set off fires and radioactive storms that would lay waste entire states.

40

Such weapons of total mass destruction had been wedded to a new delivery vehicle so swift that it virtually banished all thought of defense — the rocket. The Soviet Union and the United States both had developed rockets so powerful it would soon be possible to put men on the moon, but in wartime these vehicles would have the most deadly purpose. They could carry nuclear warheads across oceans and continents; they could deliver them on target in less than thirty minutes. Secretary McNamara's original reaction that "a missile is a missile" stemmed from his understanding of this total nuclear destructiveness. Strategically, as he saw it, missiles placed in Cuba changed only one thing: in case of war, they would cut minutes off the reaction-time allowed by a missile fired from Russia. But even this did not matter greatly; for there was no way, in a half-hour or a quarter, to protect oneself against the nuclear barrage once those firing buttons were pushed.

It was against this background of possible nuclear horror that the President's advisers met on Wednesday morning, October 17. New U-2 flights had produced further photographic evidence. The pictures showed twenty-eight launch pads in various stages of construction; and, for the first time, missiles themselves were visible.

Intelligence experts informed the committee that two kinds of missiles were going into place. One was a missile with a 1,000-mile range that could be installed in just a few hours and fired from a movable launch pad that could then be shifted elsewhere. The other was a 2,200-mile intermediate-range missile that would have to be fired from a fixed site. Together, the two kinds of missiles could shower some forty nuclear warheads on targets in the United States as far west as Wyoming and Montana.

How soon would these deadly weapons be ready? The intelligence community estimated that at least sixteen and possibly thirty-two missiles would be in position and ready for firing in about one week. This meant that there was some time left for action, but not much. Whatever action was to be taken would have to be taken soon.

It was the job of the members of ExCom to put the best choices before the President. Several alternatives were discussed, but most were dismissed. By the time this Wednesday discussion ended, the battle lines were drawn between two major proposals. One was the military's favorite: a surprise air strike to "take out" the missile sites. The other was to impose a sea blockade — or a "quarantine," as it became known — to prevent the shipment of further missiles into Cuba.

The hawkish group who wanted to attack at all costs included Paul Nitze, McNamara's Assistant Secretary of Defense, who had joined the group after the first meeting; General Taylor, speaking for the Joint Chiefs; Secretary of the Treasury Dillon; former Secretary of State Dean Acheson, a hawk from the Truman administration; and John McCone, the CIA chief who had just returned from the West Coast.

Those who favored some less drastic course and who were therefore inclined to favor the sea blockade included Secretary McNamara, George Ball, and Roswell Gilpatrick. Ambassador Llewellyn Thompson, who had just returned from Moscow, added words of caution. He knew Khrushchev, and he warned that Khrushchev could be excitable and impulsive. If attacked, he might just trigger a nuclear war.

The hawkish, military faction heaped scorn on the blockade proposal. How, they asked, could a blockade remove the missiles

already in Cuba? How could it stop work on the missile sites? It was an example of "closing the barn door after the horse had gone," they said, and they also saw other dangers in the plan. If we stopped Soviet ships on the high seas, they argued, wouldn't we be in a direct confrontation with Russia in any event? And if we blockaded Cuba, wouldn't the Russians respond by cutting off Berlin?

Secretary of Defense Robert McNamara. (Wide World)

These were hard questions which were not easy to answer. But the military's clamor for a sudden, devastating air strike had its dangers, too.

Secretary McNamara pointed them out. As the discussions progressed he had changed his position. He now recognized that the missiles in Cuba represented an entirely new threat to the nations of the Western Hemisphere and that action would have to be taken. But he argued that we — the United States — should

44

begin not at the top of the scale of force, but lower down the ladder, applying only limited pressure at first. This would give the other side time to reflect, to draw back; if they did not, we could step up the pressure, and then go to all-out force if we had to.

This astute reasoning made McNamara the principal and most eloquent advocate of the blockade strategy. He differed from his own deputy, Paul Nitze, because he estimated the danger of nuclear war differently, and he was more skeptical about the effects of the air strike. The military was fond of picturing this as a swift "surgical" operation. But *would* it be? McNamara pointed out that not even the Joint Chiefs were certain they could make a clean sweep — taking out all the missiles, all the bombing planes at one blow. And if they didn't get them all, if just a few missiles were left, some surviving Russian soldiers might trigger a response that would send an American city up in smoke. Defense Secretary McNamara further said that even the Joint Chiefs themselves theorized that their "surgical" air strike would have to be followed by invasion, which might mean that thousands of Russians, Cubans, and Americans would be killed; it meant war. While we might eventually have to go that route, McNamara emphasized, we should at least try other measures first.

Under Secretary of State George Ball, who later in the Johnson administration was to question the military's premises in Vietnam, followed up McNamara's thrust by attacking the air-strike proposition from another angle. A great nation, he felt, should be true to its traditions. It simply was not in accord with American practices to pull a Pearl Harbor-type sneak-attack on a tiny nation like Cuba. If we did this, we would violate our

45

own most precious traditions. Regardless of the military outcome, the world would despise us — and we ourselves would be the ultimate losers. This cogent argument struck a responsive chord in Robert Kennedy. He startled many in the room by declaring flatly: "My brother is not going to be the Tojo of the 1960s."

It was a remark that brought on a heated clash with former Secretary of State Dean Acheson. Cultured, brilliant, a hard-liner from the Truman days, Acheson was for all-out military action

At a meeting earlier in the year, Secretary of State Dean Rusk (left) confers with Vice-President Johnson, Attorney General Kennedy, and the President. (UPI Photo)

at once. The President, he said, "had the responsibility for the security of the people of the United States and of the whole free world," and "it was his obligation to take the only action which could protect that security." And that meant destroying the missile sites. Robert Kennedy, though he had perhaps an exaggerated respect for Acheson, took up the challenge. As he later wrote:

"With some trepidation, I argued that, whatever the military and political arguments were for an attack in preference to a blockade, America's traditions and history would not permit such a course of action. Whatever military reasons he and others could marshal, they were nevertheless, in the last analysis, advocating a surprise attack by a very large nation against a very small one. This, I said, could not be undertaken by the United States if we were to maintain our moral position at home and around the globe. Our struggle against Communism throughout the world was far more than physical survival — it had as its essence our heritage and our ideals, and these we must not destroy."

With Robert Kennedy so strongly opposed to a sudden air attack, opinion began to form behind the sea blockade proposal. On Thursday morning, October 18, Dean Rusk finally took a stand, opposing the military chiefs and also advocating the naval blockade. But the Joint Chiefs, convinced that only force would do the trick, would not give up.

President Kennedy was briefed each day. Sometimes he met a couple of times a day with committee members after they had finished their discussions. The military took advantage of these meetings to press their views on the President. General Curtis LeMay, then Air Force Chief of Staff, told the President bluntly that only a military attack could do the job.

*President Kennedy discusses the Cuban crisis with Air Force Chief of Staff
General Curtis LeMay and members of his staff. (Wide World)*

In one session, the President asked General LeMay what he
thought the Russians would do. LeMay replied confidently that
they would do nothing. The President, however, was skeptical.
He had just been reading Barbara Tuchman's *The Guns of*

August, with its devastating account of the origins of World War I. That tragic war, which no one had really wanted, had been brought about by just such military misjudgments — namely, that "the other side" would do nothing. And so, speaking of the present Russian position, the President told LeMay:

"They, no more than we, cannot let these things go by without doing something. They can't, after their statements, permit us to take out their missiles, kill a lot of Russians, and then [themselves] do nothing. If they don't take action in Cuba, they certainly will in Berlin."

The President's attitude was becoming clear. By Thursday evening, it seemed, a decision had been reached. The United States would try the blockade approach; we would try to make Khrushchev see reason. But the military was not ready to yield, and the Russians had yet one more deceitful trick to play.

Deceit and Decision

Throughout these tense and trying days, President John F. Kennedy played a role before the world that would have done credit to the most skillful actor. He kept to his normal routine, making the wry quips for which he was famous, acting as though he had only the customary daily cares of the presidency on his mind.

On that first Tuesday of crisis, he addressed some five hundred editorial writers and radio and television commentators at a foreign policy conference in the State Department. He reflected on the nuclear threat that hung over the world. The United States must protect itself and its vital interests, he said, without "the beginning of the third and perhaps the last war." He also commented: "It is rather ironical that the two strongest countries in the world, the Soviet Union and the United States, are the two countries which today live in the greatest danger."

But these were simply general reflections; he had said much the same thing before. He gave no hint that the world stood at the brink. Only at the close of his speech did he refer to the burdens he was carrying by reciting this bit of poetry:

> *Bullfight critics row on row*
> *Crowd the enormous plaza de toros,*
> *But only one is there who knows,*
> *And he is the one who fights the bull.*

With those parting lines, President Kennedy left his critics laughing.

On Wednesday the President kept an old promise, going up to Connecticut to campaign for his friend, Abraham Ribicoff, who was running for U.S. Senator. In New Haven, on the still generally conservative Yale campus, some students booed him and held up a placard reading: "More courage, less profile." (This was a taunt based upon Kennedy's Pulitzer prize-winning collection of historical essays, *Profiles in Courage*.) The President, a Harvard man, took it lightly, and again he left them laughing with these words:

"I have come back to this center of learning in order [applause] . . . to come back to my college, Yale [applause], and I have enjoyed the warm reception I've gotten from my fellow Elis as I drove into the city. But they will learn, as this country has learned, that the Democratic Party is best for them as it is for the country."

It was all a marvelous piece of acting by a man whose every waking hour was shadowed by the knowledge that he must make one of the most crucial decisions in the history of the world. It was an act designed to keep everyone in the dark, especially the Russians, until Kennedy had decided on his course. He was especially concerned lest some leak alert Khrushchev and give him the opportunity to serve the United States with an ultimatum before we could serve him with one.

Everything depended on keeping the initiative, and so well was the secret kept that the Russians, unsuspecting, stepped into the bear trap and exposed themselves. Long before the missiles had been discovered, arrangements had been made for the Soviet

51

foreign minister, Andrei Gromyko, to see the President on the afternoon of Thursday, October 18.

It was an awkward situation. The President would have preferred to cancel the meeting, but to do this would arouse suspicion. He decided he would have to receive Gromyko just as if he knew nothing — just as if he had no special cares on his mind.

The Soviet foreign minister, a man who certainly must have known the situation, arrived at the White House promptly at 5 P.M. He settled himself into an overstuffed chair facing Ken-

President Kennedy poses with Soviet Foreign Minister Andrei Gromyko (right) in the White House. Llewellyn Thompson, former ambassador to Russia, is at center. (Wide World)

nedy's wooden rocker, and proceeded to take the same deceitful line Khrushchev had been uttering for months.

Gromyko said the U.S. should stop threatening Cuba. All Cuba wanted was "peaceful coexistence"; she had no designs on other countries in the Western Hemisphere. Gromyko said that Premier Khrushchev had instructed him to tell President Kennedy that Russia was supplying Cuba only with equipment for agriculture and land development — and a small amount of defensive weapons. Gromyko said he also wanted to stress that Russia would never, under any circumstances, put offensive weapons into Cuba.

The President, as Robert Kennedy later wrote, was "astonished" at Gromyko's boldness. He was also angered. The President was tempted for a moment to expose the lie and the liar, but he kept a tight rein on himself. He told Gromyko that it was not the United States, but Russia, that was responsible for the discord and agitation in Congress and the American press because it was Russia that was supplying arms to Cuba. Again, in the most emphatic terms, Gromyko repeated his assurance that the only arms given the Cubans were "defensive." Gromyko said he wanted to stress this word "defensive" and to assure the President that none of these weapons would ever be a threat to the United States.

President Kennedy, stern now, called for a copy of his September 4 warning to the Russians and read Gromyko the passage that stressed how serious the situation would be if offensive missiles were ever placed in Cuba. Afterward, American officials wondered what Gromyko must have thought of this, but apparently, at the time, he attached no special significance to it. He evidently thought the President was simply playing a diplomatic word game with him, and he again assured Kennedy that the United States need never worry, that Russia would never do what the President was suggesting.

"I came by shortly after Gromyko left the White House," Robert Kennedy wrote later in *Thirteen Days*. "The President of the United States, it can be said, was displeased with the spokesman of the Soviet Union. . . ."

That same evening, while Gromyko was being feted by Dean Rusk in the eighth-floor State Department dining room, the members of ExCom were meeting just a floor below to hammer out a final decision. During the week, as it became clear that no course of action was without its hazards, most of the advisers had changed sides, some more than once. McGeorge Bundy, the White House adviser, had first favored a diplomatic approach, then toyed with the idea of doing nothing, and finally settled in the camp of the air-strike advocates. Secretary of the Treasury Dillon, after first favoring the air strike, joined the blockade-first group. "What changed my mind," he said later, "was Bobby Kennedy's argument that we ought to be true to ourselves as Americans, that surprise attack was not in our tradition."

By 9:15 that Thursday night, the majority of the committee had decided to back the sea blockade proposal, and they went to the White House to give the President their recommendation. The meeting lasted until after midnight, and under the President's probing questions, some men began to waver again. But in the end, it seemed, a decision had been reached. The President endorsed the blockade strategy and instructed Ted Sorensen to begin writing a speech that he could give to the nation Sunday night.

The following morning the President, keeping to his normal

schedule, departed for a round of campaign speeches in the Mid-
west. He left in a bad humor, his departure delayed for a half
hour because the Joint Chiefs of Staff had been at him again.
They simply were not willing to accept the decision that had apparently been reached on Thursday night; they pleaded in the
strongest terms for an air strike or invasion — or both.

After the President left, the members of ExCom reassembled
— and almost at once the decision of the previous night was
ripped apart. Theodore Sorensen protested that the President
had made his decision — that the debate should not now be re-
opened. But the hawks would not accept this. They again denounced the blockade as a feeble gesture. Take out the bases in
one swift, clean operation, they argued. It was a test of wills,
someone said, and let's have a showdown now. It was now or
never, another argued; we must hit the bases before they became
operational. If a decision was made at once, the Air Force could
strike on Sunday morning (just as the Japanese had at Pearl
Harbor).

It seemed not to matter to the military men that the President had already decided against them. The wrangling began all
over again. Men shifted their positions again as the hazards of
any course they might take weighed upon them. Where there
had seemed to be agreement on Thursday night, there was virtual
chaos on Friday morning. Finally, the committee divided into
two groups to write opposing position papers, one arguing for
an air strike, the other for blockade. By Friday night, most of the
committee had returned to the Thursday position, favoring a
blockade as offering the best hope of avoiding nuclear war.

Robert Kennedy telephoned the President in Chicago to
cut short his political tour and come back to Washington. The

55

committee, he said, had done all it could do; it was up to the President to make the final decision.

In Chicago, the President now developed one of the most famous colds of modern times — an illness necessary to cover up the real reason for his hasty return to the capital. On Saturday morning, his press secretary, Pierre Salinger, handed reporters what purported to be a medical bulletin on the President's mysterious condition. It read: "Slight upper respiratory (infection). 1 degree temperature. Weather raw and rainy. Recommended return to Washington."

The President got back to the White House at 1:40 P.M. and went for a swim. Robert Kennedy sat on the side of the pool and brought him up-to-date on what had happened in his absence. At 2:40 a formal meeting of the National Security Council was convened in the Oval Room. Here all the old arguments were repeated. Secretary McNamara presented the blockade position paper; Dean Rusk supported him. But the hawks were not ready to yield; they argued just as fiercely as ever for an air strike.

"One member of the Joint Chiefs of Staff, for example, argued that we should use nuclear weapons, on the basis that our adversaries would use theirs against us in an attack," Robert Kennedy later wrote in *Thirteen Days*. "I thought, as I listened, of the many times that I had heard the military take positions which, if wrong, had the advantage that no one would be around in the end to know."

By now, the President had listened to all the arguments he intended to hear. His mind was made up. He was going the blockade route. He told the military that he might have to adopt their tactics in the end; that he wanted planes and ships and men

Rare photo of military chiefs leaving Chief Executive's White House office after high-level conference. From left: General Earle Wheeler, General Curtis LeMay, Admiral George Anderson, Secretary of the Army Cyrus Vance, and presidential naval aide. (Wide World)

ready to strike at a moment's notice. But for the present he wanted to keep the options open. He wanted to give himself some room to maneuver — and he wanted to offer Khrushchev the same chance.

And so, on the following Monday night, October 22, he delivered the television speech that was to send shivers of apprehension across the civilized world.

The Mounting Crisis

The speech that rocked the world was delivered in the face of continuing and determined opposition. The military, overruled again and again, simply would not give up. Early on Sunday morning, before the President and Mrs. Kennedy went to mass, they were back in the White House, arguing as fiercely as ever for the only remedy their minds would accept — an air strike.

Secretary McNamara, Robert Kennedy, General Maxwell Taylor, and many Air Force officers were present. The President listened once more to the familiar arguments. Then he turned to General Walter C. Sweeney, commander of the Tactical Air Force, and asked him whether an air strike would take out *all* the missiles in Cuba.

Sweeney had to hedge. He estimated that 90 percent of the missiles could be destroyed, but he could not guarantee 100 percent. It became clear that the "clean, surgical" operation on which the military had harped for so long was a practical impossibility. If 10 percent of the missiles were left operational, some American cities could die, Kennedy said, and he was not going to take that risk unless he had to.

Late on Monday, before the President delivered his televised speech, he met with Congressional leaders. It was another stormy session. The hawks had their devoted followers in Congress; and many, as Robert Kennedy later wrote, were "sharp in their criticism" of the President. Senator Richard B. Russell (D., Ga.), chairman of the Senate Armed Services Committee and one of the most powerful men in Congress, proclaimed that "he could not live with himself if he did not say in the strongest possible terms how important it was that we act with greater strength than the President was contemplating." Senator J. William Fulbright (D., Ark.), chairman of the Senate Foreign Relations Committee and the most outspoken opponent of the Bay of Pigs folly, surprised the President by recommending strong military action. As Robert Kennedy wrote, the hostile session "was a tremendous strain" upon the President, and he "was upset by the time the meeting ended."

Despite such pressures, the President held firm to what he considered the more prudent course. He delivered his prepared speech, informing the world that it was poised on the abyss of nuclear disaster, but at the same time giving Khrushchev a chance to reconsider.

What would Khrushchev do? How would he react? Those were the vital questions, and the world waited in suspense for the answers.

America, in the meantime, was not idle. Actions were pressed on several fronts. The State Department showed our photographic evidence to diplomats from countries in the Western Hemisphere, and the Organization of American States backed the U.S. unanimously. The British were informed, first among our allies; and Dean Acheson was sent on a personal mission to Europe to brief President Charles de Gaulle of France and Chancellor Konrad Adenauer of West Germany. Neither hesitated. De Gaulle said he did not even need to see the photographic evidence; he was confident a great nation like the

Just in case. Above, U.S. Army antiaircraft units unlimber missiles at Key West, Florida, against trouble in the Cuban missile crisis. Below, a Navy picket destroyer patrols waters off the Florida Straits. (UPI Photo; Wide World)

U.S. would not have taken so serious a step unless it was necessary. Tell President Kennedy, he assured Acheson, that France stood with America all the way.

While these diplomatic moves were being made, American strength was being massed. The Atlantic fleet was at sea, ready to intercept Russian vessels bound for Cuba. The Air Force gathered its squadrons on southern airfields, ready to strike. An invasion force was assembled, ready to move at a moment's notice.

Even in this grim situation, there was one note of comic relief. U.S. military experts observed with surprise that Castro's generals had not dispersed his air force. Fighter planes were massed wing-tip to wing-tip on Cuban airfields, ideal targets that could be taken out at one stroke. President Kennedy said nothing, but he had a private suspicion that the American military men might possibly be as imprudent as their Cuban counterparts regarding security measures. So, unknown to the Air Force, he ordered General Taylor to send a U-2 plane over *our own airfields* to check on dispositions. The flight showed U.S. planes massed wing-tip to wing-tip just like the Cuban planes — sitting ducks in case of an enemy strike. The President reprimanded the military, and the red-faced Air Force brass ordered a wider dispersal of American planes for safety's sake.

The tensions suffered during those trying days are perhaps best illustrated by a simple anecdote. On that fateful Monday night after President Kennedy delivered his speech, George Ball did not go home; instead, he went to sleep on the davenport in his office in the State Department. He was wakened early Tuesday morning by the sound of approaching footsteps. As he roused himself, he saw Dean Rusk standing there, smiling as he had not smiled in many days.

"We have won a considerable victory," the Secretary of State said. "You and I are still alive."

Meanwhile, the unpredictable Premier Khrushchev had not responded irrationally; he had not pushed the nuclear button.

At 4 P.M. that same Tuesday, Ambassador Adlai Stevenson denounced the Soviet Union before the United Nations Security Council in New York. In some government circles, there had been doubts about Stevenson's stand on the situation. The U.N. ambassador, at one point during the week-long secret discussions, had advocated offering Khrushchev a "deal." We might agree to take our Jupiter missiles out of Greece and Turkey, or perhaps even give up the Guantanamo Naval Base in Cuba, in return for the removal of the Cuban missiles, he had suggested. Since the Jupiters were now obsolete and unnecessary, President Kennedy had previously ordered their removal; and when the Cuban crisis arose, he had been considerably irritated at the discovery that nothing had been done and his orders had been ignored. But he was also irritated at the Stevenson proposals. He felt it would be a mistake to offer Khrushchev anything, or to display any sign of weakness, lest the Russians get the false impression we were less determined than we actually were to get the missiles out of Cuba. Stevenson's proposals, some of which had also been suggested by others during those think-tank days, had been rejected. However, there was some doubt among the hawks, who later were to smear Stevenson's reputation by picturing him as a softheaded appeaser, about just how tough he would be with the Russians in the U.N.

63

U.N. Ambassador Adlai Stevenson (opposite page) and Soviet Ambassador Valerian Zorin (above) during their famous interchange at the Security Council meeting in October. (UPI Photo)

Stevenson quickly demonstrated he could be very tough indeed. He was never more eloquent than he was on that Tuesday, October 23, when he presented the American case to the United Nations. Flanked by photo interpreters and intelligence analysts, he described the hard photographic evidence that demonstrated beyond question the presence of Russian missiles in Cuba. In the midst of his speech, Stevenson received word of the unanimous OAS endorsement of the American position; and he paused in the delivery of his prepared text, flourished the

UNITED STATE

OAS resolution under the noses of the Russian delegation, and then read its text into the record on a triumphant note.

The Russians were shocked. They had hoped to split the countries of the West, but they had not succeeded. They had been caught like a burglar with his hands in a cracked safe, and world opinion was swiftly uniting and massing against them.

Stevenson gave them no chance to recover. On Thursday, October 25, he was back on the U.N. floor again, taunting Valerian Zorin, the Russian ambassador. Zorin had accused the U.S. of making "false accusations"; he had denied that the Soviet Union had "set up offensive armaments in Cuba." All right, said Stevenson, challengingly, then let U.N. experts inspect the missile sites. Zorin objected. And Stevenson defied him in this exchange:

STEVENSON: All right, sir, let me ask you a simple question: Do you, Ambassador Zorin, deny that the USSR has placed and is placing medium and intermediate-range missiles and sites in Cuba? Yes or no? Don't wait for the translation. Yes or no?

ZORIN: I am not in an American courtroom, sir . . .

STEVENSON: You are in the court of world opinion . . . .

ZORIN: . . . and therefore I do not wish to answer a question that is put to me in the fashion that a prosecutor does. In due course, sir, you will have your reply.

STEVENSON: . . . I am prepared to wait for my answer until hell freezes over . . . .

It was a magnificent performance. The Russians were being exposed before the world. But the issue of nuclear war, of life or death, still teetered in the balance. The question was still, as it had been from the first: What would Khrushchev do?

Challenge at Sea

Twenty-five Russian ships, some with those suspiciously wide hatches, were plowing through the high seas on their way to Cuba. All day Tuesday, October 23, U-2 planes charted their progress. The ships all held to their course. They kept coming — and coming.

If the Russians defied the American blockade, if the United States had to use force and some of their ships were sunk, if Russians were killed, it almost certainly meant war. U.S. intelligence services detected an extraordinary number of radio messages flashing back and forth between Moscow and the ships, but the signals were in code and we did not know what they said. Our only clue was the actions of the ships themselves, and the ships kept coming on as if the Russians were determined.

Hoping to impress upon the Russians the seriousness of the situation, Robert Kennedy went to see Ambassador Dobrynin in his third-floor office in the Russian Embassy. Dobrynin still insisted he had no knowledge of offensive weapons in Cuba, and many Americans concluded he was probably telling the truth; he simply did not know. Both Dobrynin and Kennedy were worried men. "As I left," Kennedy wrote later, "I asked him if the Soviet ships were going through to Cuba. He replied that that had been their instructions and he knew of no changes."

Tired, discouraged, and disheveled, Robert Kennedy went

They kept on coming. Aerial photo (above) shows typical Russian cargo ship bearing arms inbound for Cuba. (UPI Photo) SAM missile site (below) at Bahia Honda, Cuba, as photographed on October 23, 1962. (Wide World)

CANVAS COVERED MISSILE TRA
IN HOLD REVETMENT

NET COVERED LAUNCHERS

BULLDOZER BURYING TANK IN REVETMENT WALL

CANVAS COVERED FRUIT SET
SURROUNDED BY VERTICAL NETTING

LE REPAIR RAMP

CANVAS COVERED MISSILE TRAILERS

to the White House and reported the details of the fruitless talk. He found the President conferring with an old friend, British Ambassador David Ormsby-Gore, who had been his dinner guest. The ambassador was concerned because the American Navy had set the point for intercepting the oncoming ships 800 miles at sea. The Navy had wanted to keep its ships beyond the range of Russian MIG fighters stationed in Cuba, but Ormsby-Gore pointed out that the 800-mile line limited the time in which the Russians could react. It meant that the confrontation at sea would come very, very soon.

"Why not give them more time to analyze their position?" he suggested.

President Kennedy saw the wisdom of the advice and ordered Secretary McNamara to pull the interception zone back to 500 miles. The President appeared cool and collected as ever, handsome, perfectly tailored. But Ormsby-Gore, who knew him well, saw the signs of an almost unbearable tension in him. He talked with unnatural rapidity, in machine-gun bursts of words. And his eyes seemed screwed up tight as if to shut out the hideous visions he saw.

The next morning piled tension upon more tension. The President and members of ExCom met — and waited. It was all they could do. Thousands of miles away, out at sea, the Russian ships kept forging ahead. It was no longer a matter of hours, only a matter of minutes, before some of them would reach the blockade zone — before action would have to be taken.

"I think these few minutes were the time of gravest concern for the President," Robert Kennedy later wrote. "Was the world on the brink of a holocaust? Was it our error? A mistake? Was there something further that should have been done? Or not done? His hand went up to his face and covered his mouth. He opened and closed his fist. His face seemed drawn, his eyes pained, almost gray. We stared at each other across the table...."

The tension in the room became almost unbearable. Then, at 10:25 A.M., a messenger brought a note to CIA Chief John McCone. He read it.

"Mr. President," McCone said, "We have a preliminary report which seems to indicate that some of the Russian ships have stopped dead in the water."

A few minutes later, at 10:32, the report was confirmed. Six of the Russian ships had stopped at the very edge of the quarantine zone and had turned back toward Russia. Others were slowing down, about to follow suit.

Dean Rusk, sitting at the President's right hand, nudged McGeorge Bundy and whispered: "We're eyeball to eyeball, and I think the other fellow just blinked."

It was the first faint indication that disaster might be avoided, that the world might survive. President Kennedy, distrusting the gung-ho attitude of the services, wanted to make certain that the Navy did not spoil it all by committing some rash act. And so he sent Secretary McNamara to see Admiral George W. Anderson, Chief of Naval Operations.

McNamara and Anderson met in the Navy Flag Plot Room, and the encounter went badly from the start. Anderson seemed to think the Navy needed no instructions; it had known all there was to know about running a blockade since the days of John Paul Jones, he said. McNamara was not to be put off. "We must discuss it," he said.

Discuss it they did — and heatedly. McNamara questioned the increasingly angry admiral about the minutest details of the

Admiral George W. Anderson, Jr., Chief of Naval Operations at the time of the Cuban missile crisis. (Photo from Cushing)

Navy's dispositions. He stressed that no vessel was to be stopped without a direct order from the President. According to some versions, Anderson at one point accused McNamara of "undue interference in naval matters." At another, it was said, the admiral waved the manual of Navy regulations under McNamara's nose and told him: "It's all in there."

"I don't give a damn about what John Paul Jones would

have done," McNamara snapped. "I want to know what you are going to do."

In the end, the secretary made his point, and Admiral Anderson huffily told him: "Now Mr. Secretary, if you and your deputy will go back to your office, the Navy will run the blockade."

Having won the first move in this world-at-stake chess game, President Kennedy exercised the greatest caution. His quarantine order had applied only to the shipment of war materiel into Cuba. Now the Russian tanker *Bucharest* was coming toward the line of blockading ships. Some wanted to stop her. But the President decided that the tanker probably carried only oil; he ordered the Navy to let her pass. An East German passenger ship with some 1,500 persons aboard was also allowed to steam on toward Cuba. Finally, a Panamanian vessel, the *Marcula,* under charter to the Russians, was stopped and searched. She had no warlike supplies aboard and was allowed to proceed. The stop and search procedure had been more symbolic than meaningful — an indication to the Russians that we were serious and that we did not want to pressure them over the brink into war.

There was still little reason for optimism. Both U-2 and low-level flights over Cuba showed that the Russians were working feverishly on the missile sites, that they would soon have some of their deadly weapons in position to fire. The United States had gained a trick on the high seas where its Navy was all-powerful, but there was still no indication that America was any closer to winning the game — the removal of Russian missiles from Cuba.

Communications between President Kennedy and Premier Khrushchev seemed to indicate, however, that the Russian leader was flustered and was doing some frantic maneuvering. He had been caught flat-footed; he had so misjudged Kennedy that he had not expected to be called to account before the world; and he was now as appalled as Kennedy was at the prospect of a nuclear war he had done so much to precipitate.

The Kremlin often moves in mysterious ways, and never did it move more deviously than now. At 1:30 P.M. Friday, October 26, John Scali, the diplomatic representative of the American Broadcasting Company, was sitting in his cubicle in the State Department's pressroom. The telephone rang. The caller was Alexander S. Fomin, a Soviet Embassy counselor, who asked Scali to meet him for lunch. Scali said he was very busy. Fomin would not be put off. "It's very important," he said. "Meet me at the Occidental in ten minutes."

Scali went to the restaurant on Pennsylvania Avenue; and there, to his astonishment, he suddenly found himself a player in one of the highest-stakes poker games in modern history. For Fomin made a startling proposal. He suggested to Scali that the missile crisis might be settled on these terms:

1.   The Russians would dismantle the missile sites and ship the missiles back to the Soviet Union under U.N. supervision.

2.   Fidel Castro would promise never to accept and install offensive weapons in the future.

3.   The United States would promise never to invade Cuba.

Fomin urged Scali to take this proposal back to the State Department, and he added that, if Adlai Stevenson pursued this line in the United Nations, he would find Ambassador Zorin interested.

John Scali, American Broadcasting Company reporter at the time of the Cuban missile crisis, holds up a copy of the note written by Secretary Rusk in response to the Russian peace feeler. Reporter Scali relayed it on to the proper source. (Wide World)

Scali hurried back to the State Department with his momentous message. American officials were as astounded as the reporter. What did it mean? They finally concluded that Fomin could hardly have taken such action on his own. His message must be a feeler, another indication that perhaps Khrushchev was trying to find a way out of the trap he himself had set. Deciding to treat the Fomin overture seriously, Dean Rusk composed this message for Scali to take back:

"I have reason to believe that the USG [United States Government] sees real possibilities in this and supposes that representatives of the two governments could work this matter out with U Thant [Secretary-General of the U.N.] and with each other. My impression is, however, that time is very urgent."

Scali repeated this message, word for word, to Fomin in the coffee shop of the Statler Hilton Hotel at 7:35 P.M. Fomin asked: "Does this come from the highest source?" Scali answered: "Yes." Fomin insisted: "Are you absolutely certain?" And Scali replied that he was. At this, Fomin rushed off, saying he had to get in touch at once with the highest authorities in Moscow.

The Fomin-Scali maneuver coincided with another development. At 6 o'clock on this same Friday night, a long message from Premier Khrushchev to President Kennedy began to come in over the teletype linking the State Department with the American Embassy in Moscow. It was a long, rambling message, filled with emotion and horror at the prospect of the universal death and destruction that would be caused by a nuclear war. By turns, it threatened and pleaded. There was no reason, Khrushchev said, for us to interfere with any Russian ships bound for Cuba, for they carried no missiles: the missiles were already in Cuba. It was the first time he had officially admitted this.

Khrushchev attempted to justify his actions. He had sent the missiles to Cuba because the U.S. threatened to invade. The weapons were there only for the protection of the Cubans. Then came this vital passage:

"If assurances were given that the President of the United States would not participate in an attack on Cuba and the blockade lifted, then the question of the removal or destruction of the missile sites in Cuba would then be an entirely different question."

It was not quite an offer — but almost one. It was a suggestion in line with Fomin's three-point plan. A sigh of relief went up from American officials. It looked as if the worst was over, as if the world would survive.

But by Saturday morning, October 27, everything had changed. And suddenly the most desperate moment of all was at hand.

The Final Crisis

Two events on Saturday morning shattered the prospects for peace that had seemed so bright on Friday evening. First, a second message, entirely different in tone, came through from Khrushchev. Second, Major Rudolph Anderson, one of the two U-2 pilots who had discovered the missile sites, had been shot down and killed by Russian SAMs during another flight over Cuba.

In planning for all foreseeable developments, American officials had agreed that if one of our planes was shot down, we would retaliate by attacking the SAM sites. Now it had happened. Shocked and angry, the members of ExCom, hawks and doves alike, were in almost unanimous agreement that we should attack the next morning. But again President Kennedy pulled back; he did not want to take such a final, irreversible action.

"It isn't the first step that concerns me," he said, "but both sides escalating to the fourth and fifth step. . . .We must remind ourselves that we are embarking on a very hazardous course."

But what other course was there? The second Khrushchev message — cold, hard, formal — changed all the conditions of agreement that had seemed so close the night before.

"We will remove our missiles from Cuba, you will remove yours from Turkey . . . ," it said. "The Soviet Union will pledge not to invade or interfere with the internal affairs of Turkey; the U.S. to make the same pledge regarding Cuba."

The Russians were bargaining now, trying to place America in the same position as themselves in world opinion because it had those antiquated missile sites in Turkey. The President was angry. He was perfectly willing to take our useless missiles out of Turkey (and he was enraged that his previous orders had been ignored and this had not already been done); but he wasn't willing to yield to a threat. The Russians had posed that threat in Cuba. They would have to remove it before anything else could be done. It looked like the final deadlock.

The Joint Chiefs of Staff, joining the conference, were practically licking their chops. This was just what they had expected, they said; this was just what they had tried to tell the President all along. There was only one thing to do: launch an air strike Monday morning.

The President was not yet willing to go that far, but no one else seemed to know quite what to do. It was at this point that Robert Kennedy proposed a solution — one so simple, so brilliant, so ingenious that it seemed to offer the only way out. Why not ignore Khrushchev's latest mesage? he said. Why not respond to the first one, as if *that* represented the true proposal?

President Kennedy agreed to try it, and Theodore Sorensen and Robert Kennedy drafted the letter. In it, the President acted as if Khrushchev had made a firm offer in the Friday night message, something the Soviet premier had not quite done. The President said he "welcomed" Khrushchev's statement of his desire "to seek a prompt solution to the problem." If the Russians would cease work on the missile sites immediately, a solution could be reached on the terms that Khrushchev himself seemed to have proposed in his Friday letter.

The President spelled out the requirements: the removal of

78

the Cuban missiles; the lifting of the American blockade once this was done; a pledge by the United States not to invade Cuba. In closing, the President expressed his hope that such a settlement would ease world tensions and would lead to further discussions aimed at "reducing tensions and halting the arms race." But the President emphasized that nothing could be done unless work was halted on the Cuban missile sites and the missiles themselves removed.

While this message was being dispatched to Moscow, President Kennedy and Secretary Rusk conferred and decided that Robert Kennedy should again contact Ambassador Dobrynin. Time was now definitely running out. The first medium-range missiles were in place in Cuba; the longer, intermediate-range weapons soon would be. Unless there was an agreement, the U.S. would have to strike soon.

This was the grim message that Robert Kennedy delivered to Dobrynin when they met in the attorney general's office at 7:45 that Saturday evening. Kennedy also emphasized to the Russian diplomat that the shooting down of Major Anderson's U-2 over Cuba was a very serious development that brought us closer than ever to the brink of war. If there should be another attack of this kind on our planes, we would hesitate no longer; we would simply have to shoot back.

Then Robert Kennedy delivered a virtual ultimatum, which he later summarized in these words:

"We had to have a commitment by tomorrow that those bases would be removed. I was not giving them an ultimatum but a statement of fact. He should understand that if they did not remove those bases, we would remove them."

Dobrynin asked what kind of a deal we offered. No deal,

Robert Kennedy said. But he then explained that the President had previously ordered the removal of missiles from Greece and Turkey, and he was angry that it had not been done. If this present crisis could be solved, Kennedy said, he felt certain that it would not be long before the President saw to it that his previous orders were carried out and the missiles removed.

After the conference, Robert went back to the White House and reported to his brother. Neither was very hopeful. The Russian line seemed to have hardened; war seemed closer than ever. Preparing for what seemed almost inevitable, the President ordered up twenty-four troop-carrier squadrons of the Air Force Reserve, ready to carry invasion forces, if necessary, on Monday morning.

Sunday dawned, a golden October day, and American officials looked at the bright sunshine and wondered whether they would live to see other days like it. Then, shortly after 9 A.M., a bulletin began to come through from Moscow.

Khrushchev had accepted the President's proposals. The crisis was over.

In the White House, the President met with his brother. He recalled how Abraham Lincoln had gone to Ford's Theater, where he was assassinated, to celebrate the end of the Civil War. Jokingly, the President said:

"This is the night I should go to the theater."

Then both he and his brother laughed.

Final Lessons of the Missile Crisis

The effects and the lessons of those thirteen days of high crisis were profound. One effect, little realized at the time, was the impact on the younger generation. On college campuses, in high schools and grade schools, a whole generation faced for the first time the horrible possibility that they and their world might cease to exist on the morrow.

"The whole campus seemed under a weird spell, hushed, numb," says a former college student who will never forget those thirteen days of October. "Everybody was shocked that anything like this could happen. People walked around the campus like robots. They walked with their heads down; they didn't even want to talk to each other. Nothing seemed real. A few went wild — live it up today because we may not be here tomorrow. This is where, I think, a lot of kids gave up on the system. If the world could end tomorrow, what were we there for? What was the use of college? Of anything?"

The long-range significance of moods like this is almost impossible to assess. But is it any wonder that a generation so shocked by the vision of instant obliteration — a generation soon to be confronted with the folly of the futile Vietnam war — turned into a generation of protest?

On higher levels, in the topmost councils of government, the lessons were many and important. The later Vietnamese war, brought on in part by President Johnson's acceptance of the kind of military, hawkish advice Kennedy had rejected, showed that perhaps the most important lesson of the missile crisis had been only imperfectly learned. In the missile crisis the military had had only one answer to everything — air strike, invasion, war; they had hardly considered that our action would cause a reaction; they had all but dismissed the idea that the Russians, attacked and humiliated, would attack in turn.

President Kennedy believed the military was blind to these obvious dangers; and so, from the first, he had drafted a strategy based on the idea that the other side must never be driven into a corner in which it had only one choice — war. Once the crisis had passed, with Khrushchev's Sunday message, he insisted on taking the same high road, avoiding any hint of triumph that might discredit his Russian antagonist. He publicly praised Khrushchev's "statesmanlike decision" as "an important and constructive contribution to peace." And he sternly warned everyone in government that there must be no crowing over victory, no humiliation of the foe.

Yet the President had been disturbed by the military's attitude, and he continued to be disturbed about it. A few weeks later, the President mused over the choices we had had as he talked to Arthur M. Schlesinger, Jr., the historian and White House aide. "If we had invaded Cuba . . . ," he said, "I am sure the Soviets would have acted. They would have to, just as we would have to. I think there are certain compulsions on any great power."

On December 17, 1962, in a joint interview with reporters from the three major television networks, the President reflected again on the perils of the nuclear age. "One mistake can make

The crisis is past. Above, an American destroyer inspects a Soviet freighter outbound from Cuba. Below, the Soviet ship Kasimov *steams away from Cuba with oblong crates of missile equipment aboard. (UPI Photo; Photo from Cushing)*

this whole thing blow up," he said. Moreover, he added that a crisis like the Cuban missile crisis could not be repeated many times without the inevitable mistake occurring that would send all mankind over the final brink.

The essence of John Kennedy's reasoning throughout the entire confrontation was contained in one simple sentence in the speech he delivered at American University in the early summer of 1963. He said:

"Above all, while defending our own vital interests, nuclear powers must avert those confrontations which bring an adversary to the choice of either humiliating defeat or a nuclear war."

In such an age, when total destruction in a major war is a distinct reality, both the President and his brother had been appalled by the narrow view of the military. As Robert Kennedy afterwards wrote, they "seemed to give little consideration to the implication of the steps they suggested." He added:

"They seemed always to assume that if the Russians or the Cubans would not respond or, if they did, that a war was in our national interest. One of the Joint Chiefs of Staff once said to me he believed in a preventive attack on the Soviet Union. On that fateful Sunday morning when the Russians answered they were withdrawing their missiles, it was suggested by one high military adviser that we attack Monday in any case. Another felt that we had in some way been betrayed."

Discussing this attitude with Arthur Schlesinger, the President himself commented that "an invasion would have been a mistake — a wrong use of our power. But the military are mad. They wanted to do this. It's lucky for us we have McNamara over there."

The final lesson, then, in such a crisis as the Cuban one —

and the most important of all — is the necessity for strong civilian control over the military. For the military demonstrated in the missile crisis that it saw war as the only solution to political and diplomatic problems. And in the nuclear age it is just this kind of blind militarism — the short-sighted thinking that produced the miscalculations that led to World War I — that could very well produce World War III and the extinction of mankind. As President Kennedy himself said during the missile crisis, referring to Barbara Tuchman's *The Guns of August,* he wanted to do his best not to create a situation that would give some writer in the future, if anyone survived, the opportunity to write *The Missiles of October.*

Thanks to the President's own firmness and restraint, thanks to the skill and vision of Robert Kennedy, he succeeded. The military had been held in check — and the world had been saved. It was a formula to bear in mind for the future, a vital formula for the survival of man in the nuclear age.

Index